Steck-Vaughn Company

Executive Editor	Diane Sharpe
Senior Editor	Martin S. Saiewitz
Design Manager	Pamela Heaney
Photo Editor	Margie Foster

Proof Positive/Farrowlyne Associates, Inc.
Program Editorial, Revision Development, Design, and Production

Consultant: Jane Powers Weldon, Project Coordinator, *The New Georgia Guide*

Published by Raintree Steck-Vaughn Publishers, an imprint of Steck-Vaughn Company.

Cover Photo: Atlanta by © Ken Biggs / Tony Stone Images

A Turner Educational Services, Inc. book. Based on the Portrait of America television series by R. E. (Ted) Turner.

Library of Congress Cataloging-in-Publication Data

Thompson, Kathleen.
    Georgia / Kathleen Thompson.
        p.   cm. — (Portrait of America)
    "Based on the Portrait of America television series"—T.p. verso.
    "A Turner book."
    Includes index.
    ISBN 0-8114-7330-9 (library binding).—ISBN 0-8114-7435-6 (softcover)
    1. Georgia—Juvenile literature. I. Title. II. Series: Thompson, Kathleen.
Portrait of America.
F286.3.T45   1996
975.8—dc20   95-38248
                                                  CIP
                                                  AC

Printed and Bound in the United States of America

2 3 4 5 6 7 8 9 10 WZ 04 03 02 01 00

Acknowledgments
The publishers wish to thank the following for permission to reproduce photographs:
P. 7 Georgia Department of Industry, Trade, & Tourism; p. 8 Atlanta Convention and Visitors Bureau; p. 10 © David Kominski/Georgia Department of Natural Resources, Historic Preservation Division; pp. 11, 12 Georgia Historical Society; p. 13 Georgia Department of Industry, Trade, & Tourism; p. 14 The Bettmann Archive; p. 15 New Echota State Park/Georgia Department of Industry, Trade, & Tourism; p. 16 The Bettmann Archive; p. 17 Little White House State Historic Site; p. 18 Atlanta Historical Society; p. 19 National Portrait Gallery; p. 20 Atlanta Committee for the Olympic Games; pp. 21, 22 UPI/Bettmann; pp. 24, 25 © Jimmy Walker; p. 26 © Uniphoto; p. 28 (top) © Ken Krakow/American Textile Manufacturers Institute, Inc., (bottom) Georgia Department of Industry, Trade, & Tourism; pp. 29, 30 (both), 31 Georgia Department of Industry, Trade, & Tourism; p. 32 Library of Congress; p. 33 Georgia Department of Agriculture; p. 34 Georgia Department of Industry, Trade, & Tourism; p. 36 (top) New Echota State Park/Georgia Department of Industry, Trade, & Tourism, (bottom) Georgia Department of Industry, Trade, & Tourism; p. 37 (top) Georgia Department of Industry, Trade, & Tourism, (bottom) © Turner Entertainment Company; p. 38 Atlanta Historical Society; p. 39 Georgia Department of Industry, Trade, & Tourism; p. 40 UPI/Bettmann; p. 41 © Reg Parker/City of Atlanta; p. 42 Georgia Department of Industry, Trade, & Tourism; p. 44 (top) Georgia Department of Industry, Trade, & Tourism, (bottom) Georgia Department of Agriculture; p. 46 One Mile Up; p. 47 (top left) © Vireo, (top right) © Virginia Twinam-Smith, (bottom) One Mile Up.

STECK-VAUGHN

PORTRAIT OF AMERICA

Georgia

STECK-VAUGHN

PORTRAIT OF AMERICA

Georgia

Kathleen Thompson

A Turner Book

RSVP

RAINTREE
STECK-VAUGHN
PUBLISHERS
The Steck-Vaughn Company

Austin, Texas

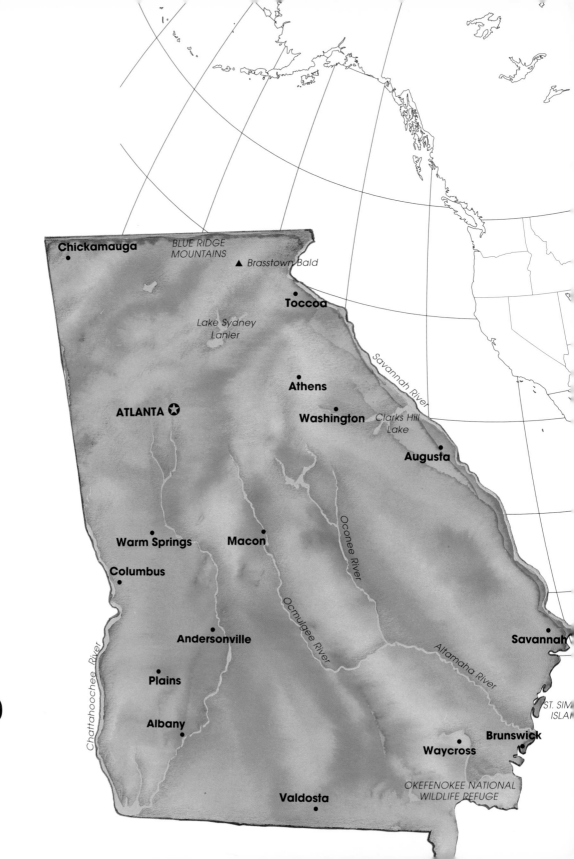

Georgia

Chickamauga

BLUE RIDGE
MOUNTAINS

▲ Brasstown Bald

Toccoa

Lake Sydney
Lanier

Savannah River

Athens

ATLANTA ✪

Washington

Clarks Hill
Lake

Augusta

Oconee River

Warm Springs

Macon

Columbus

Ocmulgee River

Andersonville

Altamaha River

Savannah

Plains

Chattahoochee River

Albany

ST. SIM
ISLA

Brunswick

Waycross

OKEFENOKEE NATIONAL
WILDLIFE REFUGE

Valdosta

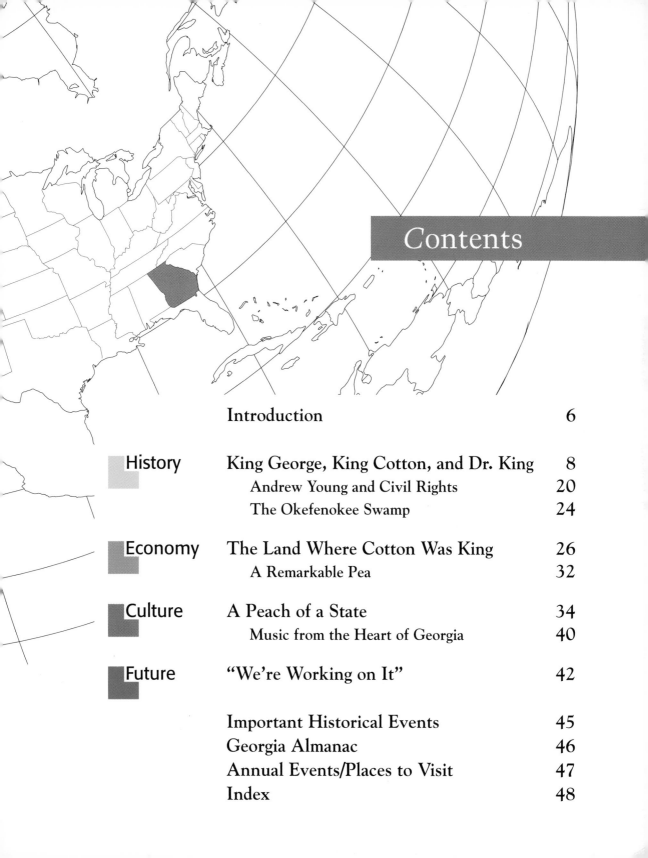

Contents

Introduction

Blessed with rich soil, heavy forests, and a mild climate, Georgia has many natural gifts. It is the nation's number one producer of peanuts and pecans, and is a leading producer of peaches. So you might think of Georgia as a farming state. But the state's main economic strength is in its industrious people. Georgia's population works hard. From blue-collar workers to computer programmers to real estate salespeople, Georgians provide the services people need. While its gentle coastal breezes lull vacationers from all over, its bustling population keeps Georgia moving ahead.

Cumberland Island is the largest of the islands that lie just off Georgia's coast. Forest covers more than forty percent of the island.

Georgia

ches, Sea Islands, plantations

King George, King Cotton, and Dr. King

Long before the Confederacy and the Civil War—as early as A.D. 1000—there was another confederacy of Native Americans who lived and farmed in the southeastern United States. These early inhabitants were sometimes called the Woodland Native Americans. These people developed towns that were organized in a pattern, much like that of many European villages. In the center was a town square, or plaza, with a meeting house. Fields of crops were planted around the outskirts of the town.

We sometimes call these people Mound Builders because they built earthen mounds that were several stories tall and had flat tops. Some of these were burial mounds. Other mounds may have been part of the Woodland religion. There are even effigy mounds, which are built in the shapes of animals.

Later, two Native American groups migrated to present-day Georgia—the Creek and the Cherokee. These people were living in the area in 1526 when a short-lived Spanish colony was set up at the mouth of

Three leaders of the Confederacy—Robert E. Lee, Stonewall Jackson, and Jefferson Davis—have their likenesses carved into the side of Stone Mountain in DeKalb County.

the Waccamaw River in what is now South Carolina. This colony was probably the first European one in what would become the United States. However, the colony was abandoned. Later, in 1540 the Spanish explorer Hernando de Soto led a group of explorers into the Georgia region from Florida. He was looking for gold. De Soto claimed the area for Spain, even though he didn't set up any permanent settlements.

When the French started to explore the region, the Spanish got a little nervous. So, in 1565 the Spanish built their first permanent settlement in St. Augustine, Florida. Next, they established missions on the string of islands along the Georgia coast. French explorers, however, continued to investigate the area.

Spain was competing with England, as well as France, for territory in present-day Georgia. For about the next one hundred years, the Spanish had to fight off English and French pirates. These pirates attacked the Spanish ships all along the coast of Georgia.

England, which already controlled much of the territory to the north, was extending its control farther south. In 1663 Charles II of England granted land to several groups of people. That land lay between Virginia and the northern boundary of Spanish Florida.

In 1732 King George II of Great Britain granted James Edward Oglethorpe, a British general and member of Parliament, a charter for a new colony. The colony was to be located between the Savannah and the Altamaha rivers. Oglethorpe wanted to accomplish two goals for the colony. One goal was to set up a military fort to intimidate the Spanish. The other goal

This statue was found buried in one of the mounds built by Native Americans more than six thousand years ago. Some mounds were used as burial grounds and places of worship.

was to establish a place for some of Great Britain's poor to start a new life.

In 1733 Oglethorpe and over one hundred British colonists arrived at the Savannah River. They were met by Tomochichi, a Creek chief whose people lived in the area. Tomochichi helped the colonists get settled. He also convinced other Creek groups to allow the colonists to settle. More than four thousand settlers came to Georgia in the first twenty years of the colony.

In 1739 war broke out between Great Britain and Spain. By 1742 Oglethorpe defeated the Spanish at St. Simons Island. Most of the Spanish threat to British territory in Georgia was now over.

In spite of help from the Creek, the colony did not prosper. The settlers complained of not having a voice in the government. Others demanded slaves to help them grow crops. The problems became too numerous for Oglethorpe and his group, so they gave up their charter. In 1752 Georgia became a royal colony.

When the Revolutionary War began in 1775, the thirst for independence struck quickly. Georgia's citizens forced the royal governor to flee. In 1776 Georgia's delegates to the Continental Congress—Button Gwinnett, Lyman Hall, and George Walton—voted in favor of independence. These men also signed the Declaration of Independence for Georgia.

In 1778 British forces captured Savannah. The British eventually seized all of Georgia except for Wilkes County, northwest of Augusta. The British

James Oglethorpe, founder of Georgia, brought only 35 families with him when he started the colony.

were finally driven out in 1782. The war ended a year later. In 1788, Georgia became the fourth state to ratify the new Constitution of the United States.

After the war, cotton became an important product in the South. But growing the crop and preparing the cotton for market required much hard work and many people. Most Georgian farmers used slaves from Africa who were imported from the West Indies. Once the cotton was ready to harvest, workers had to remove the cotton seeds from the cotton fibers—which was hard to do. Harvesting cotton was a very time-consuming and expensive job.

In 1793 Eli Whitney invented the cotton gin on a plantation near Savannah. (The word *gin* was short for "engine.") The cotton gin revolutionized agriculture in Georgia and other southern states. Whitney's new machine did the separating quickly and mechanically. Suddenly cotton became a very profitable crop. Settlers started new cotton plantations all over the

This photo was taken in the 1800s. There was no age limit for cotton field workers.

state. More slaves were brought in to do the hard labor required to grow the crop. Cotton was king.

In 1795 Georgia was larger than it is today. At one time, Georgia stretched from the Atlantic Ocean to the Mississippi River. Today, that region west of the Chattahoochee River makes up almost all of two states, Alabama and Mississippi. In 1795, a group of land companies used dishonest means to get this land. The companies bribed the Georgia legislature to pass a special law. That law said that the companies could buy the land for about one and a half cents per acre! Because the Yazoo River ran through part of the land, the event was called the Yazoo Fraud.

The people of Georgia were upset when they found out about the sale. They elected a new legislature that repealed the bill, but it was too late. Many of the new owners refused to give up their land. Finally,

Sequoyah's Cherokee syllabary has 86 "letters." Each represents an individual Cherokee syllable.

Georgia sold all its land west of the Chattahoochee River to the federal government. The government promised to settle the Yazoo claims.

The Yazoo Fraud was the result of Georgians' desire for more land. Mainly, they needed the land because so many people wanted to start cotton plantations. In an effort to gain more land, the government agreed to remove all the Native Americans from Georgia. By 1827 the Creek had sold all their lands in Georgia and moved to Arkansas.

Moving the Cherokee was more difficult. This group had mixed many European customs into their own civilization. The Cherokee had developed towns. A Cherokee named Sequoyah had developed a system of writing, and the people had established a Cherokee newspaper. The group also had a system of courts and judges similar to the American system of justice. The Cherokee system even included a supreme court.

The Cherokee tried desperately to satisfy the Georgians' desire for land, while holding off total removal. The Cherokee signed treaties and argued within the American judicial system. They even took their case to the United States Supreme Court.

Finally, in 1838 United States troops rounded up all the Cherokee and forcibly removed them to Oklahoma. About seventeen thousand Cherokee were forced

to walk the entire distance. Some of them knelt down and kissed the ground as they started to leave. Others broke from the group and wrapped their arms around nearby trees. Such was the love these people had for their homeland. Four thousand Cherokee died along the way. This exodus has become known as the "Trail of Tears."

For the next 12 years, Georgia cotton planters expanded their plantations. Such large farms needed slave labor to be efficient. In 1860 Abraham Lincoln was elected President of the United States. Lincoln was morally opposed to the institution of slavery. Because southern states were so dependent on slavery, they began to withdraw from the Union. Georgia was the fifth state to leave. In 1861 the Civil War began.

Georgia was right in the middle of the war. The Confederates won a major battle at Chickamauga on September 19 and 20, 1863. In 1864 Union General William Tecumseh Sherman invaded Georgia and

General William Sherman's troops surrounded Atlanta and cut it off from the rest of the Confederacy from September to November. He then continued his march from Atlanta to Savannah.

captured Atlanta. He then moved southeast toward the Atlantic Ocean. Sherman had two goals. He wanted to cut the supply lines that supported Confederate troops. He also wanted to break the Confederates' will to fight. As he and his troops marched from Atlanta to Savannah, they destroyed almost everything of military and economic value. They cut a pathway sixty miles wide.

Sherman reached Savannah on December 22. He then turned north, marched through South Carolina, and finally joined the Union forces in Virginia. The strategy was successful. A few months later, the war was over.

Georgia was readmitted to the United States in 1868, but it was expelled again in 1869. The state would not approve the Fifteenth Amendment to the Constitution, which allowed African American men the right to vote. Finally, in 1870 the state ratified the amendment and was readmitted to the Union.

Much of Georgia was destroyed during the war. What's more, Lincoln's antislavery policy freed the slaves. There was no money to hire workers, so the cotton plantations failed. As a result the Georgian landowners designed a system called sharecropping. In this system, plantation owners divided their land into small farms. Workers and their families rented the smaller farms and grew crops. The owners, in turn, sold the crops and paid a small percentage back to the farmers. But the owners kept so much of the profits that the tenant farmers were very poor. Poverty became widespread.

Georgia moved away from a one-crop economy slowly and painfully. By 1900 some industries had developed, producing mostly cloth and wood products. Some farmers began to grow peaches, nuts, corn, and tobacco, but most still grew cotton. In the 1920s a plague of boll weevils destroyed most of the cotton crops. Georgia's economy had hit bottom.

The Great Depression of the 1930s brought even more hardship to Georgia. Millions of people across the country were out of work. The national economy was at a standstill. Franklin D. Roosevelt became President in 1933. Within the first one hundred days of his administration, Roosevelt instituted his New Deal programs. These programs helped Georgia and other states build highways, public buildings, and drainage systems.

World War II brought the United States out of the Depression. The country went back to work by building materials for the war effort. Defense industries and military training camps grew in Georgia. Farm workers moved to the cities to take jobs in factories.

In 1943 Georgia became the first state to give 18-year-olds the right to vote. Two years later, the poll tax was outlawed. This tax required a payment in order to vote. Most poor people could not afford this tax. Since many African Americans were poor sharecroppers, they were unable to vote in any election.

The 1950s and the 1960s in Georgia were a time of racial integration. Georgia had a very large African

In 1924 Franklin D. Roosevelt, who had polio, began to spend several months of each year at Warm Springs, Georgia. Three years later, Roosevelt founded the Georgia Warm Springs Foundation to provide inexpensive treatment for people who have polio.

American population and a very deep history of discrimination. Now, it became the birthplace of the civil rights movement. Dr. Martin Luther King, Jr., and other members of the Southern Christian Leadership Conference led the nation toward equality for all.

In 1965 Julian Bond, an African American civil rights leader, was elected to the Georgia House of Representatives. The other members of the House refused to admit Bond as a member. The reason they gave was that he opposed the United States' involvement in Vietnam. In 1966 the U.S. Supreme Court declared that Bond should be admitted.

Since the beginning of the civil rights movement, African Americans have become a significant force in Georgia's cities. Georgia has produced African American leaders such as Andrew Young, once a United States congressman and later an ambassador to the United Nations. In 1973 Maynard H. Jackson, Jr., was elected mayor of Atlanta. He was

Dr. Martin Luther King, Jr., was born and raised in Atlanta. He's shown here in front of his boyhood home.

the first African American mayor of a large Southern city. Since then, many African Americans have become mayors of Georgia's cities.

Georgia's Governor Jimmy Carter became the thirty-ninth President of the United States in 1977. He still is active in Georgia, helping to build houses for the homeless through Habitat for Humanity. The Carter Presidential Center in Atlanta helps promote democracy and peace around the world.

As in other states, today Georgia still struggles with the remnants of its racial problems. Many of these problems are centered in urban areas. As the cities become overcrowded, more and more people have moved to the outlying suburbs. In some ways, this has expanded the cities, causing what has become known as "urban sprawl."

The end of the Cold War in the 1990s, while good news for the nation as a whole caused problems for Georgia. In areas where the economy depended on military projects, another source of income now must be found. Georgia is nothing if not adaptable, however. Its history has shown that. The Advanced Technology Development Center on the Georgia Tech campus has a way to help. The ATDC and the university are offering assistance programs to stimulate growth in Georgia's high-tech industries. Another center in Warner Robins encourages growth in the aerospace industry. A third center in Augusta specializes in biomedical products. With the help of universities and high-tech companies like these, Georgia can look confidently ahead to the new century.

President Jimmy Carter grew up on a peanut farm in Plains, Georgia. At age five, Carter sold peanuts on the streets of Plains, and as an adult, he worked as a peanut farmer before going into politics.

Andrew Young and Civil Rights

Andrew Young has an exceptional record of service to the state of Georgia and to the United States. He served in the United States House of Representatives from 1972 to 1977. He was the first African American from the South elected to the U.S. Congress since 1901. President Jimmy Carter later appointed Young to be the U.S. ambassador to the United Nations. Young also was mayor of Atlanta from 1981 to 1989.

Andrew Young spent his childhood in New Orleans, during the years when racial segregation was the law. Later he went to Howard University, an

Andrew Young was a candidate for governor of Georgia in 1990.

Andrew Young speaks at a United Nations conference.

African American university founded in 1867. Young studied to be a doctor, but after a while he decided that he really wanted to be a minister. In 1955 he was ordained as a minister in the United Church of Christ. His duties led him to Atlanta, where he has been based ever since.

Young knows what the South was like before the civil rights movement. He remembers the Georgia of that time, when racism and poverty were

As executive director of the SCLC, Andrew Young worked closely with Dr. Martin Luther King, Jr.

terrible. "But," he says, "we began to deal with problems of race. We began to deal with problems of poverty."

Andrew Young's history illustrates the important role that African American churches played in the civil rights movement in the South. He had become active in civil rights activities in Atlanta—especially in the efforts to register African Americans to vote.

Many other individuals were involved, too. Then, in 1957, Dr. Martin Luther King, Jr., founded the Southern Christian Leadership Conference (SCLC). The SCLC was created so that there would be a way to combine all these individual efforts. In fact, it has been said that Atlanta created the civil rights movement.

Young joined the SCLC in 1961 and soon became its executive director. He remembers the efforts of the organization very well. "In the process of facing head-up those kinds of difficult problems, I think we generated a new leadership that had worldwide relevance. Because every place in the world, every place, has problems of race and culture and poverty." Because of the efforts of SCLC and people like Andrew Young, the U.S. Congress passed the Civil Rights Act of 1964 and the Voting Rights Act of 1965.

Racism is part of the dark side of Georgia's history. But the struggle to overcome discrimination has become the bright side. The African American population of this state showed people all over the country and all over the world how to change things. The strong, nonviolent protest that began in Georgia became a model for citizens nationwide.

The dream of equality for all people has not been fully realized. But in the last several decades, the United States has begun to come to terms with its problems. The changes can be measured in many ways. One is the fact that in 1973, Atlanta elected Maynard Jackson, Jr., mayor. He was the first African American to become mayor of a major southern city. Andrew Young succeeded him in 1981.

The demonstrations and unrest that began in Atlanta were the beginning of the solution. It was a time when history was made in Georgia. As Andrew Young commented, "There is no city, there is no state, there is no nation that does not have problems of racial and ethnic diversity and problems between its haves and its have-nots. I don't know a state that has gone further in dealing with those problems than we have. We've still got a long way to go, but we know the problems. We know we can deal with them. And we're working on it."

The Okefenokee Swamp

Down in southern Georgia, there lies a huge swamp. But this is no ordinary swamp. It is the largest freshwater basin in the United States. It's called the Okefenokee. That name is said to come from a Seminole word meaning "land of the trembling earth." The name describes the way the land in the swamp shakes when you step on it. Why does it do that? The many tiny hummocks, or islands, of the swamp actually float on top of the water.

The Okefenokee takes up an area 25 miles by 40 miles. Most of it is now a national wildlife refuge. Hundreds of varieties of animals and plants live there, including bears, alligators, and exotic orchids. The swamp is one of the country's largest natural bird refuges.

People used to live there, too. Some people still do. Ralph Davis was born and raised on the edge of the Okefenokee. He remembered that ". . . about every mile or mile and a half, there was a family of people that lived around the swamp. Before the government bought it, we made a living out of it, taking people out there to fish and hunt."

The swampers weren't farmers. They didn't have jobs in town either. The swamp was their home and their living. They respected it in the same way the people who lived on this land hundreds of years ago did.

"It was a hard life, but it was a good life," Ralph Davis explained. He compared the lifestyle to that of Native Americans. "If they needed something, they went into the swamp and got it. They didn't try to destroy everything. They just took what they needed."

Water lily flowers in the Okefenokee Swamp may grow to be as large as one foot across.

Most of the Okefenokee Swamp is now a national wildlife refuge. Many different species of animals live there, including deer, bear, bobcats, otters, raccoons, opossums, and alligators.

They also respected the dangers of the swamp and the creatures that lived there. "Anything that gets in the water out there is groceries for that alligator," Ralph Davis forewarned. "When you're traveling through the swamp, there's a lot of eyes that are looking at you that you don't see."

Nowadays you can visit the Okefenokee Heritage Center. In nearby Waycross, you can even visit Obediah's Okefenok, the restored home of Obediah Barber. He was called the "King of the Okefenokee." There are many legends about him. One famous story tells about the time that Obediah killed a full-grown black bear—single-handedly! Some of the stories are told by the descendants of Barber's twenty children, many of whom still live in the area.

There are not many swampers left today. Those that remain are a breed apart. Living off the land and keeping peace with nature bring them a sense of pride and independence.

The Land Where Cotton Was King

Georgia is the largest state east of the Mississippi. Once, much of the land was covered with cotton plantations. The state's economy depended on growing and harvesting cotton. But that is no longer the case.

Today, cotton accounts for only a small percentage of Georgia's economy. Like most of the rest of the United States, Georgia's economy is now dominated by service industries. Wholesale and retail trades make up the biggest part of these service industries. Next come personal services, such as medical and legal services, computer services, and repair shops. These are followed by the finance, insurance, and real estate industries. Governmental services also contribute to the economy. There are several military bases in the state, including the United States Army Signal Center and a United States Navy submarine base.

Manufacturing accounts for under twenty percent of Georgia's economy. Processed foods and transportation equipment, including cars and aircraft, make up Georgia's main manufactured products. Textiles come

Besides being Georgia's capital and largest city, Atlanta is the financial and commercial capital of the southeastern United States.

At Monfort Finishing, shown here, spools of yarn are placed on a roller, which is fed through a loom or a knitting machine. The loom produces a woven fabric that is 36 to 60 inches wide.

These logs are being processed in Georgia. The southeast produces more lumber than any other region of the country.

second. Only North Carolina produces more textiles than Georgia. The textile industry produces mostly carpeting—about $7 billion worth a year. But the industry also makes cloth, yarn, and synthetic fabrics.

Along with textiles, food processing is an important industry. A big part of that processing involves food that is grown in the state. Peanut butter and peanut oil are major products. Fruit, seafood, and vegetables are also frozen and canned in Georgia factories.

Georgia is home to the famous Georgia pine tree. About 60 percent of the state's land is forest. Many of its forests are commercial forests, which means that lumber companies grow the trees specifically for processing. Processing wood from such forests is an important manufacturing activity in Georgia. Mills all over the state produce lumber, various types of paper, and other wood products.

It's clear that agriculture is not as important in Georgia as it once was. In fact, agriculture makes up only two percent of the state's gross product. But there are strong ties between Georgia's agriculture and its manufacturing, so sometimes numbers don't tell the whole story. Today, the biggest moneymaker is not cotton, but chickens. Since they are processed in Georgia, those chickens end up being an important source of economic strength. Other farm animals—hogs and cattle—are also important farm products.

Peanuts are the biggest field crop in the state. Georgia is also the nation's leading producer of pecans. Tobacco is another important source of income. Georgia's farmers also grow soybeans, sweet potatoes, cabbages, snap beans, corn, and tomatoes. They raise a variety of animal feeds, also. Georgia peaches are famous. That's why Georgia is sometimes called the Peach State. The state is also a leader in the production of watermelons.

Transportation has always been important in Georgia. General Sherman had strong reasons for fighting his way through the state during the Civil War. Georgia had an extensive network of railroads on which supplies were being delivered to Confederate troops. Sherman's march destroyed that network. But the railroads were rebuilt after the war. Today, Atlanta is a rail hub for the Southeast.

Deep-water ports are important for international trade. There are deep-water ports at Savannah and

These Georgia peaches show why the state's fruit is so well loved.

The first Coca-Cola was sold in Atlanta in 1886. It was advertised by drug stores both as a soft drink and as a medicine. Pictured here is Coca-Cola's corporate headquarters.

Tourism is a strong part of Georgia's economy. People come to see old-fashioned southern homes such as this one.

Brunswick. Georgia has a number of rivers, so the state government has increased barge service for shipping chemicals, wood, and mineral products. Air traffic is also important to Georgia's economic health. Atlanta is home to Hartsfield International Airport. More cargo planes land and take off at Hartsfield than at any other airport in the world. Only O'Hare Airport in Chicago handles more passenger traffic than Hartsfield.

The extensive transportation system is one reason that companies find Georgia attractive. In fact, many corporations have their headquarters in Georgia. Coca-Cola was invented in Atlanta by a man named John Styth Pemberton. He was a pharmacist when he made the first serving of the product. The Coca-Cola Company has its headquarters in the city. A few of the other companies with main offices in Atlanta are Home Depot, United Parcel Service, and Delta Airlines.

The land of Georgia is not only rich, it is also beautiful. Tourists want to see the pre-Civil War architecture of Savannah. Georgia is a state that satisfies curious travelers, also. The sacred mounds left behind by ancient Native Americans may create more questions than they answer. The shuddering ground and the rustic beauty of the Okefenokee Swamp provide a deep respect for natural history.

Tourists also visit Georgia's Atlantic Coast to swim and fish in the warm ocean waters.

A Remarkable Pea

Here's a riddle for you. This pea plant is called "groundnut," "ground pea," and "goober." Pound for pound it has more calories than sugar and more protein than beef. It grows in a pod that ripens under the ground. To make a favorite sandwich, you need this pea, jelly, and bread. What is it?

Did you guess the peanut? Then you're right. This plant first came to the United States on slave ships from Africa. The Bantu of Africa call the peanut *nguba.* From that word we get the peanut's popular name—goober.

Half the peanut crop grown in the United States is used for peanut butter. The rest is eaten roasted, in candies, or in cookies. In most parts of the world, peanuts are grown for their oil. Peanut seeds are nearly fifty percent oil. And peanut oil has hundreds of uses. It is used for cooking and in many sauces and dressings. It is also used to make soaps, shampoos, cosmetics, paint, and even explosives!

The rest of the peanut plant is useful, too. Peanut shells ground into a powder are used in plastics and wood substitutes. The leaves of the peanut plant make a good hay for feeding livestock. Farmers use the stalks and branches as a fertilizer for growing more peanuts.

When George Washington Carver arrived at Tuskegee Institute in 1896, peanuts were not even considered to be a farm crop.

Peanuts must be harvested at exactly the right time. If they are harvested too early, the peanuts will not have ripened, but if they are harvested too late, the stems will snap and the peanuts will stay in the soil.

Until the early 1900s, however, no one in the United States was farming peanuts. At that time, the main crop of the South was cotton. But the land was getting weak from growing too much cotton. Farmers were in trouble.

In 1896 a leading agricultural scientist, George Washington Carver, wanted to help the southern farmer. He knew that peanut plants restore nitrogen to the soil. Peanuts can grow on land where other crops will no longer grow. Through research, Carver developed over three hundred products from the peanut. Farmers began growing peanuts instead of cotton. As a result, peanuts helped the South rebuild its agricultural economy.

Today, the peanut is an important large cash crop in the southern states.

Georgia alone produces nearly half of the country's peanuts. Each year, Georgia farmers grow almost one hundred thousand tons of peanuts! There's good reason for this. Georgia offers a perfect peanut-growing environment. Peanuts need warm weather, sunshine, and no risk of frost. They grow best in sandy soil with a fair amount of rain. It takes five months for the pods to grow and ripen. At harvest, the entire plant is pulled up, so the peanut plants must be replanted annually. It takes a lot of work to grow peanuts. But Georgia peanut farmers are happy to keep up the supply. Who knows, with all those uses for peanuts, maybe someone will invent a few more.

A Peach of a State

Georgia is a peach of a state. It's known for its peaches, but that's not the only reason Georgia is special. There's a sense of history everywhere in Georgia. After all, it was one of the 13 original colonies. It also played an important role in the Civil War.

Historic buildings and architecture are everywhere you look. Colonial life is highlighted along the Georgia coast. Savannah is the site of the nation's largest Urban Historic District. Old homes and shops have been restored so that walking through them is like stepping into the state's colonial past. Near places such as Athens, Washington, Madison, and Westville, you can see restored plantation homes. Visitors get to see what it was like to live and work on a real plantation. Jarrell Plantation, near Macon, is a nineteenth-century farmstead. It exists as the family left it. It even features a working blacksmith. Have you ever wondered what life was like at the turn of the century? You'd get a pretty good idea by visiting Tifton, where

Father and son enjoy a quiet moment at Chattahoochee National Forest in northern Georgia.

35

The publishing office of the *Cherokee Phoenix* has been completely restored.

Dr. Martin Luther King, Jr., was born in this house, which was built in 1895. The house is now a National Historic Site, and it is frequently visited by tourists.

there's a restored farm from the late 1800s.

There are Civil War monuments all over the state. The Chickamauga-Chattanooga National Battlefield Park is the nation's oldest and largest military park. Andersonville, which has also become a national historic site, includes an impressive re-creation of a Confederate prison. The Battle of Resaca is reenacted at the Confederate Cemetery just outside of Resaca. Four hundred Confederate soldiers who lost their lives in 1864 are buried here.

Georgia history on display also contains much Native American culture. Near Macon you'll find the museum at Ocmulgee National Monument, the largest archaeological development east of the Mississippi. The Etowah Indian Mounds are the site of a prehistoric village that stood between A.D. 1000 and 1500. New Echota was the capital of the Cherokee Nation from 1825 until 1838. Sequoyah worked on his Cherokee syllabary in New Echota. It was also the home of the *Cherokee Phoenix*, the first newspaper ever printed in both English and Cherokee. New Echota is the site of a Cherokee special events every year.

African American culture is also celebrated throughout Georgia. Atlanta is the home of the Martin Luther King, Jr., Center for Nonviolent Social Change. Dorchester Academy was founded about 1870 by former slaves. The First African Baptist Church was founded in Savannah in 1788. It is probably the first African

There were more plantations in Georgia than in any other southern state. Large, elaborate houses such as this one were usually located in county seats or "courthouse towns." Houses in the country were simpler.

American church in the United States. The Tubman African American Museum in Macon is devoted to African American culture and celebrates the life of this famous escaped slave. Before the Civil War, Tubman led other slaves to freedom on the Underground Railroad.

If you prefer your history along presidential lines, there's Franklin Delano Roosevelt's Little White House in Warm Springs. Plains is the hometown of former President Jimmy Carter, and the Carter Presidential Center is in Atlanta.

Georgia has produced its share of writers. Margaret Mitchell spent years writing the novel *Gone with the Wind*. It is perhaps America's most famous novel. The story takes place in Georgia during the Civil War. The book was made into a very successful movie. It now ranks as an American film classic.

The movie *Gone with the Wind* was released in 1939. It may be one of the most popular movies ever made.

In new screen splendor...
The most magnificent picture ever!

DAVID O. SELZNICK'S PRODUCTION OF MARGARET MITCHELL'S

"GONE WITH THE WIND"

Winner of Ten Academy Awards

CLARK GABLE
VIVIEN LEIGH
LESLIE HOWARD OLIVIA de HAVILLAND

A SELZNICK INTERNATIONAL PICTURE · VICTOR FLEMING · SIDNEY HOWARD · METRO-GOLDWYN-MAYER INC.

Margaret Mitchell's book *Gone with the Wind* has sold over eight million copies since it was published. It is the only book she ever wrote.

Georgia has had many other famous writers who documented life in the South. Among these are Carson McCullers, Erskine Caldwell, and Flannery O'Connor. More recently, Georgia novelist Alice Walker won a Pulitzer Prize for her book *The Color Purple*.

Before 1960 there were more people living in Georgia's rural areas than in its urban areas. Country living led to a long tradition of folk arts in Georgia's culture. Many people continue to produce handmade blankets, bedspreads, and clothing, using the same techniques their ancestors did. Other folk arts, such as music and dancing, also thrive in Georgia.

Georgia culture is highly represented in Atlanta. The Atlanta Symphony is considered one of the top ten orchestras in the country. In addition, the Robert W. Woodruff Arts Center is the largest arts complex in the Southeast. There you'll find the High Museum of Art, the Alliance Children's Theater, and many other arts activities. Museums throughout the city specialize in many subjects. For instance, the Monetary Museum features the history of money in the United States. At SciTek, the Science & Technology Museum of Atlanta, visitors can experience over one hundred hands-on exhibits. These exhibits include examples of scientific technology from the past and the present.

Atlanta also boasts an impressive television and film business. The city is home to the Cable News

Network (CNN), an international cable television news station. This industry giant broadcasts reports on events all over the world. CNN is a division of Turner Broadcasting, which produces both independent television shows and feature films.

Sports are important in Georgia, too. There are professional teams in baseball, football, basketball, and hockey. The Atlanta Braves were National League Champions in 1991 and 1992, and World Series Champions in 1995. The Atlanta Knights hockey team was the first professional hockey team to sign a woman player—Manon Rheaume. Georgia also hosts the famous annual Masters golf tournament. But perhaps the most exciting sports event in recent Georgia history happened in 1996. That's when the state hosted the 100th anniversary of the modern Olympics.

Not all of Georgia's culture is on display. It runs deep in the traditions of family members, in the way they do things. Their culture could be represented in a baby's handmade blanket. Or it could be the song on the lips of a peanut farmer. Many people in Georgia feel there's no other place like it on Earth.

The High Museum of Art in Atlanta contains European and American paintings and sculpture, African art, and twentieth-century art.

Music from the Heart of Georgia

Many people who study America's popular music believe that it originated from the gospel music of the South. There's no doubt that much of that gospel music has come from Georgia.

Gospel music began in African American churches more than a century ago. In those times, music was the best way that African Americans could express their feelings about their lives. Music revealed their dreams, their hopes, their anger, and their fears. That may be why gospel music still has such an emotional quality.

Phil Walden, a music producer in Georgia, has worked with hundreds of musicians and has great respect for gospel music. He points out that many of today's American singers trace their own musical roots to gospel singing in Georgia. The list includes Ray Charles, Little Richard, James Brown, and Otis Redding. Walden stresses their importance: "It's almost impossible to measure the influence that they had and are continuing to have today on what we call contemporary pop music. It's so real and so emotional and so Georgian and so southern, what they are doing. They are products of this state's culture, of this state's heritage."

Ray Charles wrote and recorded "Georgia on My Mind," which has become his signature song.

Jazz musicians come from all over the world to play at the Atlanta Jazz Festival.

Walden's list also includes Isaac Hayes, the Allman Brothers Band, and many others. And no one should forget jazz, which also has its roots in gospel. The jazz tradition began elsewhere in the South, but this kind of music is also alive and well in modern Georgia. The Atlanta Jazz Festival is one of the nation's leading gatherings of jazz musicians.

Music is a Georgia tradition. In the mountains to the northwest, you'll find gospel along with even more traditional religious music called "shape-note" singing. On the Sea Islands off the Georgia coast, you'll find traditional folk music that is a mixture of Spanish and West African cultures.

Georgia's music seems to take sounds from all parts of the culture. It's not one kind of music or one kind of experience. It's a blend. It combines gospel, jazz, rock, pop, country—you name it.

Maybe the music is the result of something in the warm beauty of the state. Maybe it comes out of the long history of suffering. Whatever it is, it stays on your mind—just like Georgia.

"We're Working on It"

When you talk about the future of Georgia, it's probably good to remember the words of two of its famous citizens. Andrew Young said, "We've still got a long way to go, but we know the problems. We know we can deal with them. And we're working on it." And President Jimmy Carter explained, "My children will be the sixth generation on the same land. Our orientation toward the earth with the farmland and the soil has been a very great stabilizing effect in our lives. . . . The closeness of the soil, I think, . . . lets us have faith in the future."

So if you combine the philosophy of the city and the philosophy of the land, you get a good idea about Georgia's future. The heritage of the past will continue to provide guidelines for solving the problems of the future. Georgia faces many of the same problems as other states. There are conflicts between cities and suburbs. There are questions about how to make sure that everyone is well educated and healthy.

Hartsfield International Airport handles thousands of flights every day. It is one of the world's busiest transfer hubs and air terminals.

Pollution is a threat to Georgia's freshwater sources.

Modern technology has made Georgia's farming more efficient.

Many of Georgia's problems are ones the state has been dealing with for years. There are still racial problems, and economic development must be expanded so that more of the population prospers. And environmental problems are an inevitable part of the rapid industrialization that the state has been going through.

For instance, along the Georgia coast, people get their freshwater from aquifers, which are huge underground "lakes." The coastal areas are now using up their freshwater so fast that salt water from the Atlantic is beginning to seep into the aquifers. If this continues, the coastal regions will have to find another source of freshwater. The people of Georgia have to come up with creative solutions.

In cities such as Atlanta, businesses are pursuing the opportunities presented by new technology and new communications networks. These systems could benefit everyone, both businesses and employees. The challenge is to be sure that the future includes everyone. Georgians, like Jimmy Carter, are rooted in the soil and have faith in the future. And, as they say, they're working on it.

Important Historical Events

1540 Spanish explorer Hernando de Soto crosses through the Georgia region.

1732 King George II grants a 21-year charter to create the Georgia colony.

1733 James Oglethorpe arrives with his first English settlers and founds Savannah.

1739 War breaks out between Great Britain and Spain over illegal trading and a boundary dispute between Georgia and Florida.

1742 Oglethorpe and his troops stop the Spanish from landing on St. Simons Island in the Battle of Bloody Marsh.

1778 Georgia approves the Articles of Confederation on July 24. The British capture Savannah.

1782 Americans, with the help of the French Navy, drive the British out of Georgia.

1788 Georgia ratifies the Constitution and enters the Union as the fourth state on January 2.

1793 Eli Whitney invents the cotton gin near Savannah.

1795 Land companies and state legislators become involved in a land fraud scandal known as the Yazoo Fraud.

1802 Georgia agrees to sell its lands west of the Chattahoochee River to the federal government. The federal government promises to settle the land claims involved in the Yazoo Fraud.

1827 The Creek sell the rest of their lands in Georgia to the federal government and are moved to the Arkansas Territory.

1836 Wesleyan College in Macon is the first college in the world chartered to grant degrees to women.

1838 The Cherokee are forced out of Georgia by federal troops and onto a reservation in present-day Oklahoma. The evacuated land is distributed by lottery.

1861 Georgia becomes the fifth Southern state to secede from the Union.

1863 The Confederate Army wins a major battle at Chickamauga.

1864 Union General William T. Sherman burns Atlanta and marches across Georgia to capture Savannah.

1870 Georgia is readmitted to the Union.

1920 A plague of boll weevils destroys Georgia's cotton crop.

1922 Rebecca L. Felton becomes the first woman United States senator.

1943 Georgia is the first state to give 18-year-olds the right to vote.

1965 Julian Bond, an African American civil rights leader, is elected to the state House of Representatives.

1972 Andrew Young becomes the first southern African American elected to the U.S. Congress since 1901.

1973 Maynard Jackson, Jr., becomes the first African American mayor of a major southern city.

1977 Former Georgia Governor Jimmy Carter becomes the thirty-ninth President of the United States.

1980 Cable News Network (CNN) begins broadcasting from Atlanta.

1996 Atlanta hosts the one-hundredth anniversary of the modern Olympic Games.

The state flag displays the state seal and the Confederate battle flag. The state seal shows a figure holding a sword, which represents the defense of the Constitution. The date on the bottom of the seal, 1776, is the year the Declaration of Independence was signed. The banners display the state motto, "Wisdom, Justice, and Moderation."

Georgia Almanac

Nickname. The Empire State of the South; The Peach State

Capital. Atlanta

State Bird. Brown thrasher

State Flower. Cherokee rose

State Tree. Live oak

State Motto. Wisdom, Justice, and Moderation

State Song. "Georgia on My Mind"

State Abbreviations. Ga. (traditional); GA (postal)

Statehood. January 2, 1788, the 4th state

Government. Congress: U.S. senators, 2; U.S. representatives, 11. State Legislature: senators, 56; representatives, 180. Counties: 159

Area. 58,930 sq mi (152,627 sq km), 21st in size among the states

Greatest Distances. north/south 318 mi (512 km); east/west 278 mi (447 km)

Elevation. Highest: 4,784 ft (1,458 m). Lowest: sea level, along the Atlantic Ocean. Coastline: 100 mi (161 km)

Population. 1990 Census: 6,508,419 (19% increase over 1980), 11th in size among the states. Density: 110 persons per sq mi (43 persons per sq km). Distribution: 63% urban, 37% rural. 1980 Census: 5,463,087

Economy. *Agriculture*: chickens, peanuts, eggs, beef cattle, hogs, milk. *Fishing*: shrimp, crabs. *Manufacturing*: textiles, food products, transportation equipment, paper products, chemicals, clothing, electric equipment. *Mining*: clay, stone

State Bird: Brown thrasher

State Flower: Cherokee rose

Annual Events

★ King Week at the Martin Luther King, Jr., Center for Nonviolent Social Change in Atlanta (January)

★ Cherry Blossom Festival in Macon (March)

★ Stay and See Georgia at Stone Mountain Park (May)

★ Civil War Encampment at Stone Mountain Park (July)

★ Georgia Fall Festival in Hiawassee (October)

★ Georgia Peanut Festival in Sylvester (October)

★ Apple Festival at the Fairgrounds in Ellijay

Places to Visit

★ Atlanta History Center in Atlanta

★ Callaway Gardens, near Pine Mountain

★ Dahlonega Gold Museum

★ Etowah Mounds, near Cartersville

★ Historic Savannah Waterfront District

★ Lake Lanier Islands, near Buford

★ Little White House in Warm Springs

★ New Echota, near Calhoun

★ Okefenokee Swamp in south-eastern Georgia

★ Stone Mountain Park, near Atlanta

State Seal

47